Unwritten Black Girl Rules

To my friends and family, thank you for helping me bring this vision to life. And most of all, to my mother, Stephanie Mills-Lawrence for having my back through it all.

Black girls. We come in different shapes and sizes. Our melanin is phenomenal and our hair is rich in texture. But it seems like nobody understands us. The simple things we ask for that just cannot be respected. As a black girl, I understand the struggles that we must go through to be accepted and understood. From our unique styles to our unique features. We are often overlooked and always told that we complain too much. So, I took it upon myself to write about some of the unwritten black girl rules. It is about time you guys get a better understanding of our world.

P.S.
This is solely for entertainment purposes. Enjoy.

We are not aggressive

When a black woman express and asserts herself like any other woman would, she's considered to be aggressive. 9 times out of 10, we're not even being aggressive. We are just simply expressing ourselves.

When giving a compliment, just say we are pretty.

"You're pretty for a black girl." That is NOT a compliment. That's just disrespectful. It's pretty much saying black girls are ugly. Just say that we look pretty or just leave us alone.

Don't Touch My Hair

And I mean it in the nicest way possible.

When we wear our natural hair, it's not a sign of boldness

People need to understand that being natural isn't a statement but rather just the closest thing we get to being ourselves and embracing it.

Stop assuming that our hair is a weave.

Bantu knots. Curly hair. Braids. Slick ponytails. Braids. Finger waves. Curls. Straight hair. Black women different hair textures allows us to wear our hair in many different ways. It is not always a weave. Our hair pertains so much texture and definition that we can do hairstyles that looks "unrealistic."

We are not all mixed.

Us black girls have unique features. We can look Asian, black, middle eastern, etc. That does not mean that we are mixed. We come in many different forms. Asking if we are mixed is simply implying that black girls lack the features to be beautiful. My mother taught me that black women have the power to birth babies of any race.

We get it. Black girls are not your cup of tea and that is fine. BUT, STOP DRAGGING US DOWN TO MAKE YOURSELF LOOK GOOD. We don't care.

Stop telling us about you dating outside your race.

We are not all "ghetto"

This isn't just for black girls only but for all the black people. Ghetto is such a derogatory term. People who refer to black people as "ghetto" say we are loud, ignorant, all use EBT (public assistance), that we are stupid, all we do is steal, etc. But I can't count on my hands and toes how many black people are not ghetto despite coming from slum backgrounds. We do not let our history determine our future and for every time a black person breaks a barrier, we prove these people wrong.

Just because we wear weave does not necessarily make us bald.

Box braids. Frontals. Closures. Sew ins. Wigs. Lemonade braids. Goddess braids. It comes in all different styles and textures. HOWEVER, it is a protective style. Just because you see a black girl with a certain hairstyle you are not accustomed to seeing does not automatically make it a weave. Mind the business that pays you instead.

Mind your business when it comes to our hair

People love to ask 'is that your real hair? Is it a weave? A wig?' like that's going to help them to sleep at night. It's my hair. I bought it and that's that.

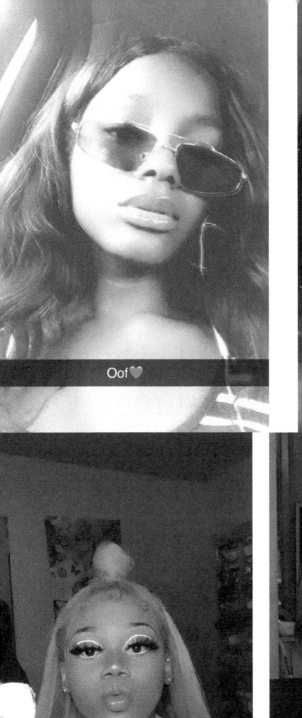

Oof 🖤

Not every black girls' father is absent in her life.

This again is for all of my black people. it is not uncommon for people that is not of color to assume that we don't know our fathers. In some cases, unfortunately it is true. But in other cases, we know our fathers who are alive and working to make sure we get what we need.

Thou shall NOT judge another woman in the beauty supply store.

When we are getting our hair done, sometimes we may run out of supplies. When we bump into each other at the beauty supply store, do not laugh. We all have our days. Just give a small smile and keep it moving.

Social media has had a way of convincing people that all black girls know how to twerk and do all of the "black" dances (i.e. the electric slide). However, there are some of us who don't know how to dance. There is nothing wrong with that. But forcing black girls to dance when they don't know how to is actually annoying. Go find yourself a hobby.

Not all of us can dance

Hair Day

For my non melanin people with the thin hair, allow me to elaborate on this rule. Hair day for my black queens is the day where we cater to our hair. Take out the hair, detangle, wash, deep condition, leave in conditioner, blow dry, air dry, and so on. So if you decide to make plans and we tell you that we're going to be doing our hair, don't think that it can be done in just 30 minutes. Our curls needs more than just some water to move on. It takes special oils and a lot of time for us to make it look as glamorous as it does. So, please respect that and postpone the plans until the next day.

They assume that because you are black that you enjoy rap and that's all you listen to. Well new flash, some of us enjoy Taylor Swift and Justin Beiber. Heck, we like us some R&B as well. Rap isn't every black girl's preference. So think twice before you put a rap song on and expect the black girl to sing along or dance to it.

We don't enjoy the same kind of music

Not all of us look the same.

For some reason, you could be out with your friends and strangers would stop you to ask if you guys are twins. You could have different facial structures, different hair, even be different shades and they must stop you to ask you a stupid question like that. It's very irritating and redundant.

We all don't have different fathers

People love to assume that just because you got the same mother that means the father is different. Just because siblings may be different shades or different features doesn't mean that they are not related.

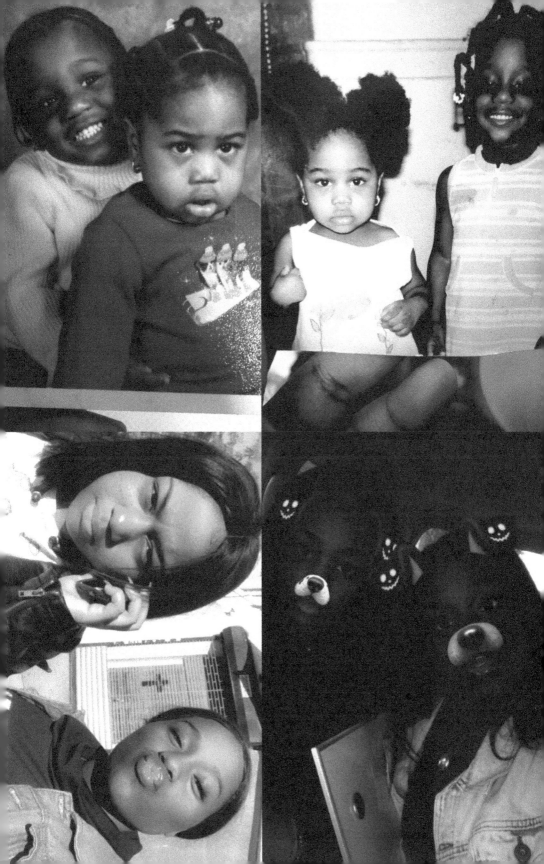

And Lastly

We are beautiful queens breaking down each barrier that comes our way, each obstacle that tries to hold us back, and each stereotype that tries to degrade us.

We are black and we are are beautiful.